# The ALL-IN-ONE APPROACH to

## Succeeding at the Piano®

 with CD

### by HELEN MARLAIS

Name: _____

Teacher: _____

Beginning Date: _____

*Let's Continue Piano Lessons!*

MOZART   HAYDN   BEETHOVEN

Production: Frank J. Hackinson
Production Coordinators: Peggy Gallagher and Philip Groeber
Editors: Edwin McLean and Peggy Gallagher
Art Direction: Andi Whitmer – in collaboration with Helen Marlais
Cover Illustration: © 2014 Susan Hellard/Arena
Interior Illustrations: © 2010 Susan Hellard/Arena &
                        © 2014 Teresa Robertson/Arena
Cover and Interior Illustration Concepts: Helen Marlais
Engraving: Tempo Music Press, Inc.
Printer: Tempo Music Press, Inc.

ISBN-13: 978-1-61928-132-5

# TABLE OF CONTENTS

## COMPOSERS AND ARRANGERS

Timothy Brown:   Student solos: p. 14, 21, 28, 40
Lyrics: p. 21, 28, 40
Duet parts: p. 14, 21, 28

Kevin Costley:   Student solos: p. 6, 32
Lyrics: p. 6, 32

Mary Leaf:   Student solos: p. 5, 10, 36, 38, 44
Lyrics: p. 5, 10, 36, 38, 44
Duet parts: p. 10, 36, 44

Helen Marlais:   Student solos: p. 3, 8, 12, 13, 23, 25, 29, 30, 33, 34, 35, 37, 42, 43
Lyrics: p. 3, 8, 13, 14, 29, 37, 39, 42
Duet part: p. 12

Edwin McLean:   Student solos: p. 17, 18, 46
Lyrics: p. 17, 25
Duet part: p. 18

Kevin Olson:   Student solos: p. 31, 41
Lyrics: p. 31, 41
Duet part: p. 41

The composers of the classical pieces are listed under the titles:
• p. 14 (*Melody by Chopin*—from *Fantasie Impromptu*—F. Chopin)   • p. 23 (*The Can-Can*—J. Offenbach)
• p. 25 (*Roller Coaster Ride*—F. Beyer-adaped)   • p. 37 (*See the Show*—F. Beyer-adapted)   • p. 43 (*Trumpet Tune*—H. Purcell)

# Book 1A—Review

- Circle the position for the R.H.:   MIDDLE C Position   TREBLE C Position
- Circle the half rests. How many are there? _____

## Andy Aardvark

CD 2, 3, 4 • MIDI 1

Scurrying along

*mf* An - dy | Aard - vark's | in a cheer - ful | mood;

He likes | ants, they | are his fa - v'rite | food.

*f* Snuf - fling | 'round, his | nose next to the | ground;

He goes out at | night, | when the moon is | bright!
*mp*   *p*

Answers: Treble C Position, 10

FJH2226

3

# We Love Notes!

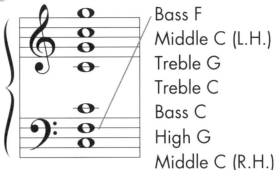

## 1. MATCHING GUIDE NOTES

- Draw a line from each guide note to its correct name.

Bass F
Middle C (L.H.)
Treble G
Treble C
Bass C
High G
Middle C (R.H.)

## 2. INTERVALS

- Draw a note **up** from each guide note. Then name the notes.

Up a 2nd      Up a 3rd      Up a 3rd      Up a 4th

Ex:

*G*   *A*

- Draw a note **down** from each guide note. Then name the notes.

Down a 3rd      Down a 5th      Down a 4th      Down a 2nd

## 3. TREBLE STAFF NOTES

- Name the notes. Then play them.
  Treble C Position:

FACE:

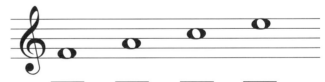

These notes are 2nds   3rds   apart. (circle one)     These notes are 2nds   3rds   apart. (circle one)

## 4. ARTICULATIONS

- Are these notes *staccato* or *legato*?

Now play them!

☐ Check the box when you are done.

_____

_____

FJH2226

# G Position

- Play and sing!

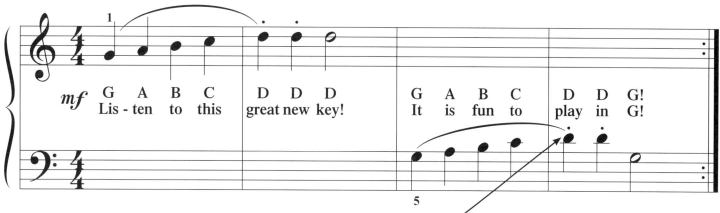

G A B C | D D D | G A B C | D D G!
Lis - ten to this | great new key! | It is fun to | play in G!

Discover a NEW NOTE!
D is a 2nd **up** from
Middle C.

Draw Middle C
and D here:
Then play this 2nd.

**Practice steps:**

- Circle the 3rds.
- Tap hands together and count.

## The Bagpiper

CD 5, 6, 7 • MIDI 2

A 2nd up from C is _____

**Merrily**

1st time:
*f*
2nd time:
*mf*

There's | a | pip - er up | on the | hill,
See | his | sil - hou - ette, | ver - y | still,

play - ing an | old Scot - tish | tune._____
plays by the | light of the | moon!_____

> **Tempo** means the speed of a piece.
> Tempo markings are often Italian words.

Here are some important ones:

**andante**
walking speed

Papa
Haydn

**allegro**
happy, spirited

Mozart

**moderato**
moderate speed

Beethoven

**adagio**
slowly

Brahms

## The Singing Violins

CD 8, 9, 10 • MIDI 3

**Practice step:**

• Which composer is moving to the tempo of this piece? (circle one)

Moderato

Vi - o - lins play
*mf*

tunes that sing;

What a love - ly
*mp*

sound they bring!

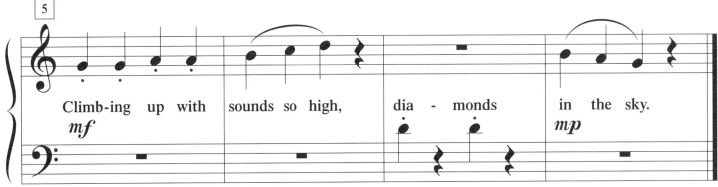

Climb-ing up with
*mf*

sounds so high,

dia - monds

in the sky.
*mp*

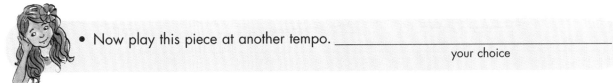

• Now play this piece at another tempo. _____
                                        your choice

FJH2226

# At the Horse Race

## Time yourself! Look at a clock!

- Write the letter name of the notes.
- Draw an X on the nearest guide note to help you.
- Then play the intervals on the piano.

Guide Notes:

G  D

_____

_____

_____

_____

_____

_____

_____

_____

_____

_____

_____

- How long did it take you to finish?
  _____ Minutes _____ Seconds

## Time to Compose:

- Make up a piece in G Position.
- Will the piece have 𝄽's? *staccato* notes? slurs?
- Choose a race for your title: *The Bike Race,*
  *At the Horse Race, The Running Race.*

My title:

_____

★ Practice your piece as many times as it
takes to remember it completely!

# The SHARP SIGN ♯

Notice the sharp sign (♯) in front of the guide notes below.
When you see a ♯, play the very next key **higher**.

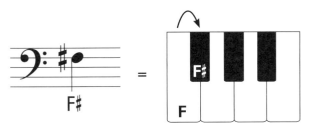 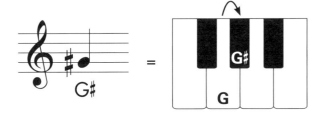

- Write the name of the notes below. Then play them.
- Circle the pattern that is played on **2 white keys**.

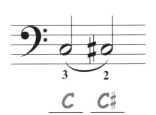

C   C♯

## Seahorses

CD 11, 12, 13 • MIDI 4

| A sharp lasts through an entire measure. |

**Andante**

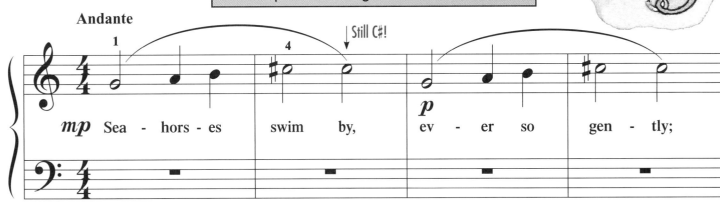

↓ Still C♯!

*mp* Sea - hors - es    swim    by,    ev - er    so    gen - tly;

*p*

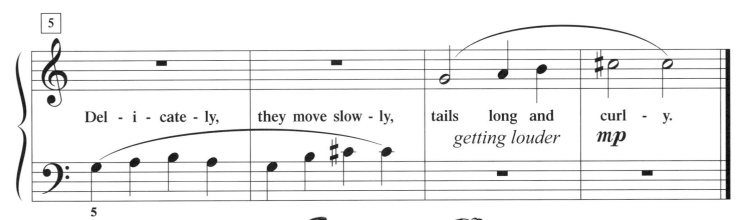

Del - i - cate - ly,    they move slow - ly,    tails    long    and    curl - y.
                                                *getting louder*              *mp*

**Note to Teachers:**
Students can use a "Tissue Box" touch release for the last note.

Chopin

- Press down the damper pedal for the entire piece.
- Keep your heel on the floor.
- How does the sound change?

FJH2221

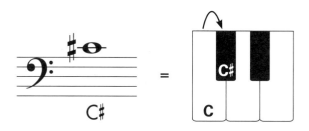

The distance between these two notes is called a **half step**.

C♯

**1.**

This key is _____♯.
Find it and play it!

This key is _____♯.
Find it and play it!

**2.**
- Name the half steps below. Then play them.
- Circle the correct keys on the keyboard below each staff.

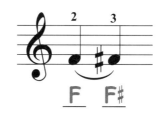

F  F♯

___ ___

___ ___

**3.**
- Add a sharp before each note. The **center** of the ♯ is **always** on the **same** line or space as the notehead.
- Then write the letter names and play the notes.

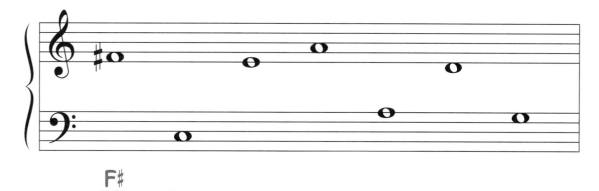

F♯  ___  ___  ___  ___  ___  ___

## Practice steps:

- Name the sharp in this piece: ___ #
- Which 2 lines of music have the same pattern of notes? _____ and _____ .

# The Pet Store

Happily

*mf* My dog and | I like to | roam the pet | store,

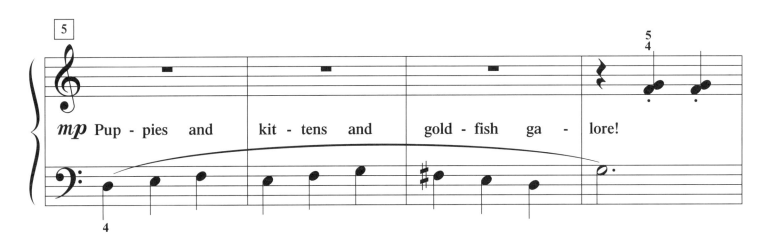

*mp* Pup - pies and | kit - tens and | gold - fish ga - | lore!

DUET PART: (student plays 1 octave higher)

FJH22

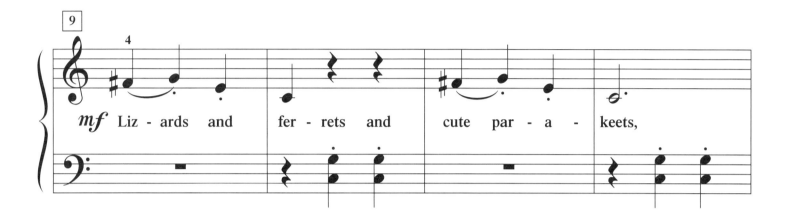

**9**

*mf* Liz - ards and | fer - rets and | cute par - a - keets,

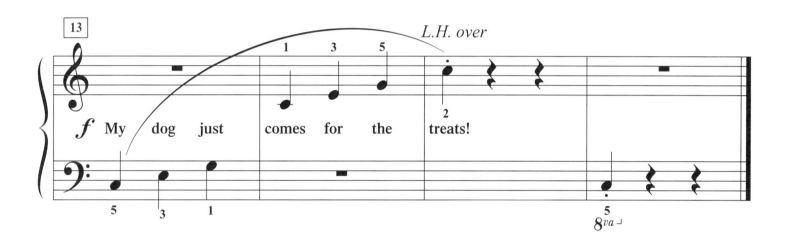

**13**

*L.H. over*

*f* My dog just | comes for the | treats!

*8va*

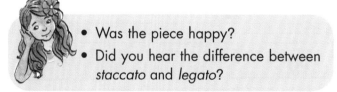

- Was the piece happy?
- Did you hear the difference between *staccato* and *legato*?

**Note to Teachers:** When playing the last note, students can push forward and off the key with their wrist. Their hand and forearm will follow their wrist. This is called a "Push Off" touch release.

## Practice steps:

- Name the sharp in this piece: ___ ♯
- Use "unit" practice (1 measure plus 1 downbeat)
  and repeat 3 times correctly.

# Scandinavian Folk Song

CD 17, 18, 19 • MIDI 6

DUET PART: (student plays 1 octave higher)

FJH2220

# The FLAT SIGN ♭

Notice the flat sign (♭) in front of the guide notes below.
When you see a ♭, play the very next key **lower**.

- Write the name of the notes below. Then play them.
- Circle the pattern that is played on **2 white keys**.

# Gloomy Days

| A flat lasts through an entire measure. |

- Which measure has the most flatted notes? measure _____

## Practice step:

- Circle the only flat in the piece.

*Frédéric Chopin (1810-1849) is one of the most famous composers of all time. He grew up in Poland, but spent most of his life in Paris, France. He wrote mostly piano music and was a pianist and teacher as well.*

# Melody by Chopin
(Frédéric Chopin)

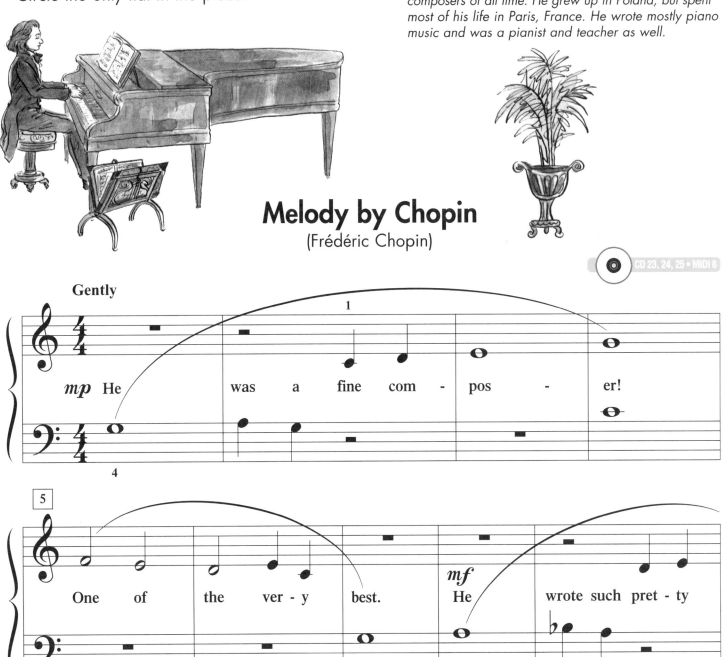

DUET PART: (student plays 1 octave higher)

FJH222

**10**

mel - o - dies; He loved pi - a - no mu - sic.

*move L.H.* ②

- Can you sing the theme*? _____
  yes

  Place a 🙂 on the line when you can!

**10**

* a theme is an important melody.

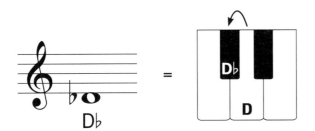

The distance between these two notes is called a **half step**.

Db

**1.**

 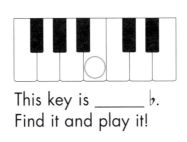

This key is _____ ♭.
Find it and play it!

This key is _____ ♭.
Find it and play it!

**2.**
- Write the name of the notes below, then play them.
- Circle the correct keys on the keyboard below each staff.

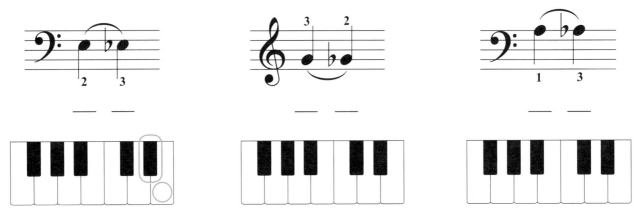

**3.**
- Add a flat before each note. The **center** of the ♭ is **always** on the **same** line or space as the notehead.
- Then write the letter names.

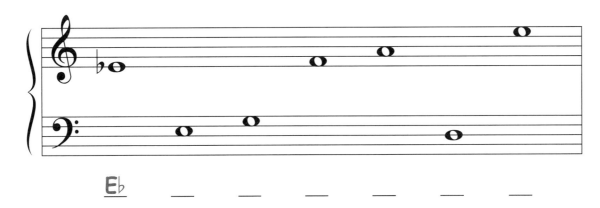

Eb ___ ___ ___ ___

FJH222

## Practice steps:

- Plan the 5ths.
- What are the two flats you will play? ____ ♭ and ____ ♭

CD 26, 27, 28 • MIDI 9

# Mountain Village

**Moderato**

mf Moun-tain vil-lage way up high, rain for-ests in the sky.

5

Friend-ly peo-ple pass-ing by, chil-dren at play.

9

mp Frogs are croak-ing in the trees, birds sing-ing in the breeze;

13

Far be-low, the dis-tant seas van-ish a-way.
*getting softer* p

A ♯ or a ♭ lasts through an entire measure but not past a bar line.
In a new measure, a ♯ or ♭ will be written again.

CD 29, 30, 31 • MIDI 10

# Jazz Steps

**Jazzily**

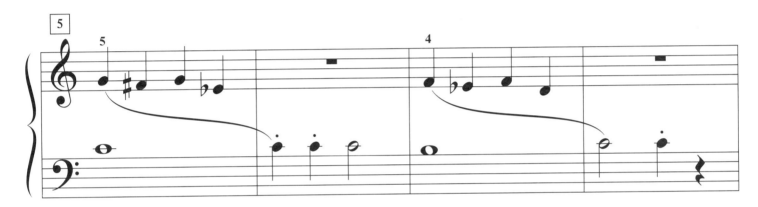

DUET PART: (student plays 1 octave higher)

FJH222

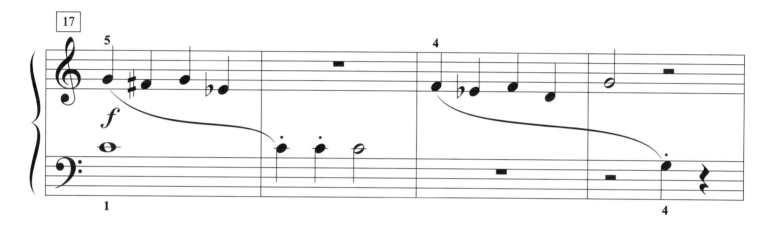

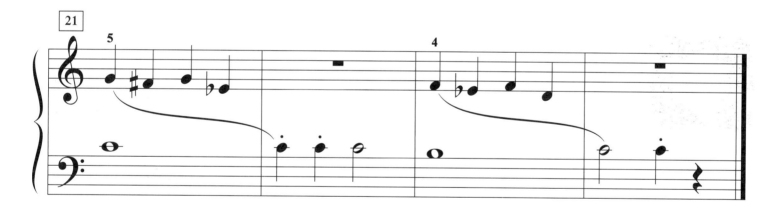

# Matching

**1.** Draw a line from each note on the staff to the correct key on the keyboard.

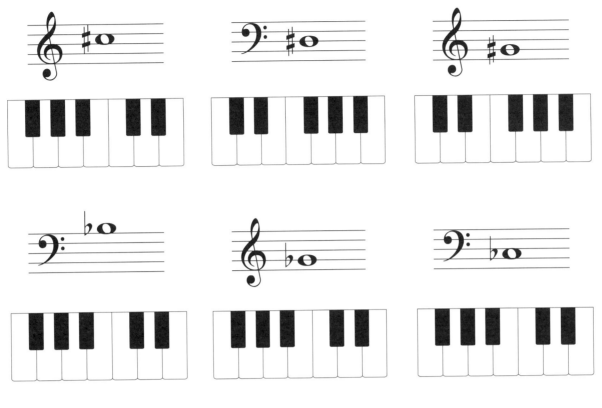

 CD 32 • MIDI 11

**2.**

## In Outer Space

- With the pedal down, play each piece.
- First time: Use arm weight to drop to the bottom of the key. Listen to the *f* sound! ——————→
- Second time: Lightly play each note. Lift your wrist gently out of each key. Use a "Tissue Box" touch release.

Drip    Drop    Roll

Next, listen to your L.H.

FJH2226

**Practice steps:**

- Tap and count.
- Then practice slowly until you know it.

# The Lazy Pup

CD 33, 34, 35 • MIDI 12

**Fast and fun**

*mf* Such a la-zy pup, he sleeps all day long;

But he'll perk right up if you play his song.

Danc-ing 'round, up and down, jump-ing to the beat. So

play his fa-v'rite song, get him on his feet!

*f*

*L.H.*

**DUET PART:** (student plays 1 octave higher)

R.H.

L.H. *mp*

*mf*

# Review of Guide Notes and Intervals

**1.** Play and say aloud these guide notes, bottom to top.

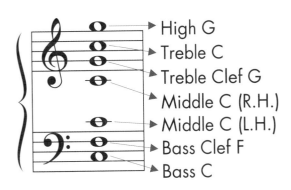

- High G
- Treble C
- Treble Clef G
- Middle C (R.H.)
- Middle C (L.H.)
- Bass Clef F
- Bass C

**Time to Compose:**

- Make up a piece using at least 3 of these guide notes.

My title: _____

**2.**
- Write the intervals and the note names.
- Find and play the patterns on the piano.

3rd up

C  E

_____

_____

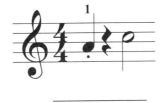

_____

_____

_____

_____

_____

**3. OCTAVE REVIEW**

- Find and play these octaves, saying the name of the notes aloud!
- Write the name of the notes.

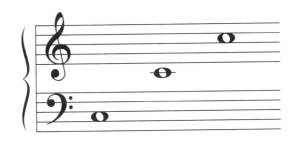

_____  _____

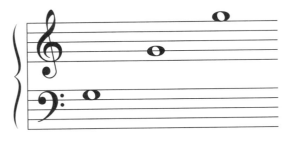

_____  _____

FJH2226

## Practice steps:

- Find one each of the following intervals:
  2nd - measure _____
  3rd - measure _____
  4th - measure _____
  5th - measure _____
- Now find and circle a **half step**.

# The Can-Can
(Jacques Offenbach)

CD 36, 37, 38 • MIDI 13

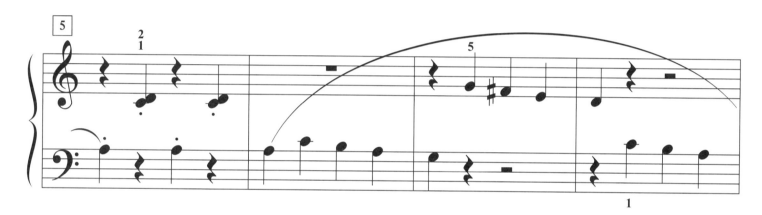

# Tonic and Dominant

Beethoven

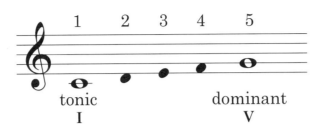

tonic
I

dominant
V

Tonic and dominant are
two important notes.

- Tonic is labeled with a I.
  Dominant is labeled with a V.
  (I and V are Roman numerals. This
  numbering system was invented by
  the Romans over 2,000 years ago.)

- I is the first note of a five-finger pattern.
  V is the fifth note of a five-finger pattern.

- The dominant is always a 5th up from tonic.

- Play these tonic and dominant notes on the piano:

*The Coliseum in Rome*

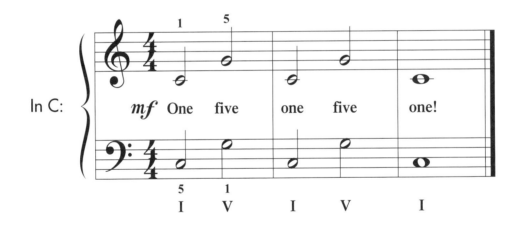

In C:

*mf* One five one five one!

I V I V I

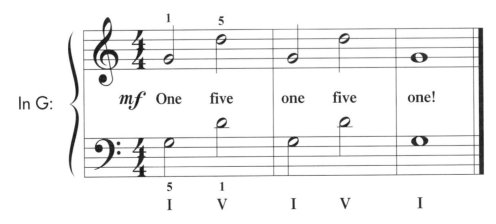

In G:

*mf* One five one five one!

I V I V I

- Play a D as tonic. What is the dominant? _____ Play it!

- Play an F as tonic. What is the dominant? _____ Play it!

(Your teacher will ask you to play others!)

# Tonic and Dominant in C

* Play and sing!

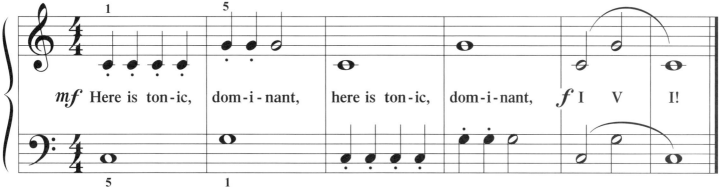

mf Here is ton-ic, dom-i-nant, here is ton-ic, dom-i-nant, f I V I!

Now, play in G Position.
You will be *transposing*.

## Roller Coaster Ride
(F. Beyer – adapted)

**Practice step:**

* Circle the dominant notes in the L.H.

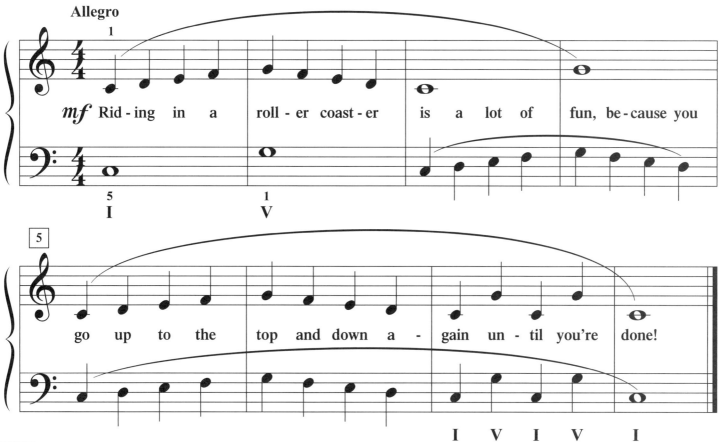

Allegro

mf Rid-ing in a roll-er coast-er is a lot of fun, be-cause you

I          V

go up to the top and down a-gain un-til you're done!

I   V   I   V   I

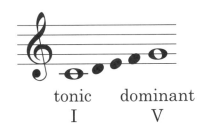

tonic    dominant
I        V

Tonic and dominant are two important notes.

 I   V

- The first note of the five-finger pattern is *always* called the **tonic**.
- The fifth note of the five-finger pattern is *always* called the **dominant**.
- The **tonic** and **dominant** are always a 5th apart.

**1.**
- Write the dominant note in each example below.
- Then play the examples.

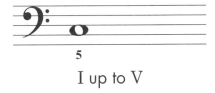

I up to V

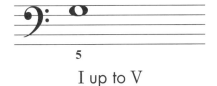

I up to V

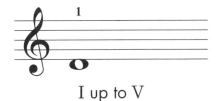

I up to V

**2.** The dominant note wants to return to the tonic.
- Write the tonic note in each example.
- Then play the examples.

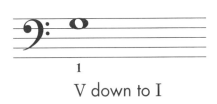

V down to I

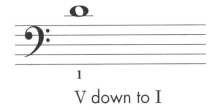

V down to I

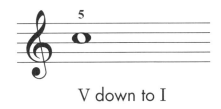

V down to I

**3.** Circle the examples that show I-V-I.

FJH2226

# Bass G

• Find and play these 4 guide notes in the Bass Staff:

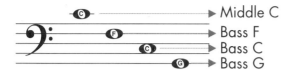

→ Middle C
→ Bass F
→ Bass C
→ Bass G

**1.** • Write the name of the notes and the intervals.

• Then play the notes!

Ex.

C   F

5th down

_____  _____

_____

_____  _____

_____

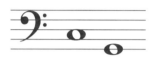

_____  _____

_____

**2.** As fast as a steam engine, do the following:

• Write the name of the notes.

• Draw a line from the note on the staff to the correct key on the keyboard.

• Then find and play each note on the piano.

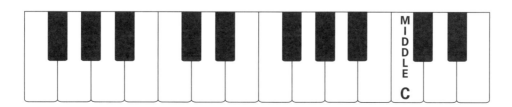

## Practice steps:

- Both hands are in bass clef!
- The R.H. plays Guide Notes Middle C and Bass F.
- The L.H. plays Guide Notes Bass C and Bass _____.

 CD 43, 44, 45 • MIDI 16

# Jamaican Boat Song

**With spirit**

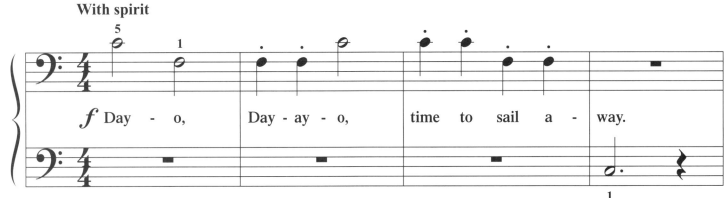

_f_ Day - o,  Day - ay - o,  time  to  sail  a - way.

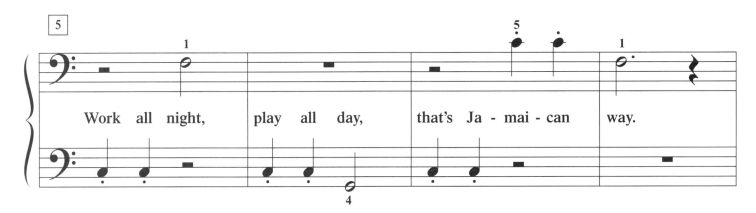

Work  all  night,  play  all  day,  that's  Ja - mai - can  way.

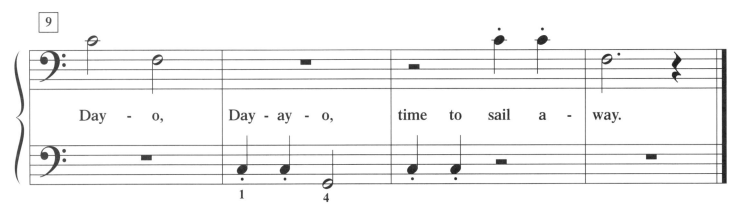

Day - o,  Day - ay - o,  time  to  sail  a - way.

DUET PART: (student plays as written)

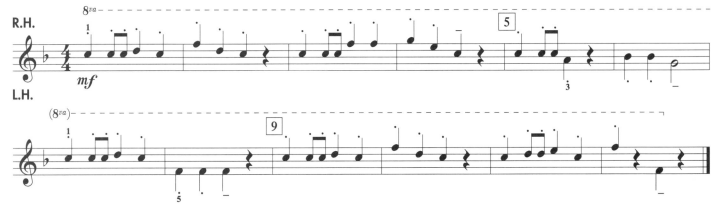

28

FJH222

## Practice steps:

- Tap hands together and count aloud.
- Circle the 4ths.
- How many Bass G's are there? _____

# The Smiling Hippopotamus

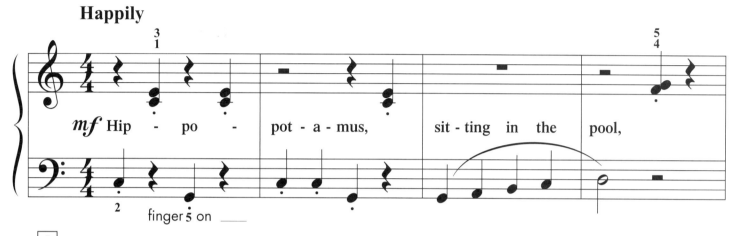

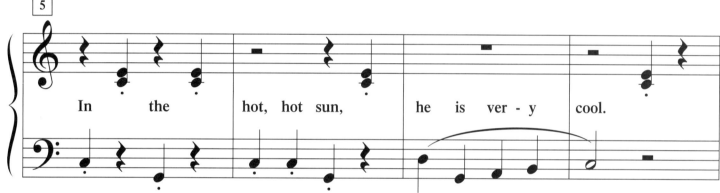

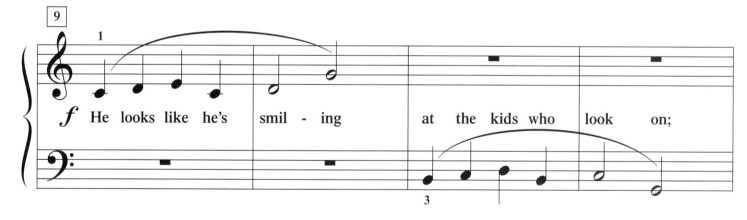

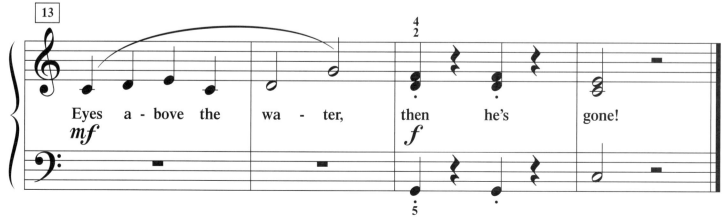

# Dynamics

*crescendo*      *diminuendo*

means to gradually get louder (stronger)

means to gradually get softer

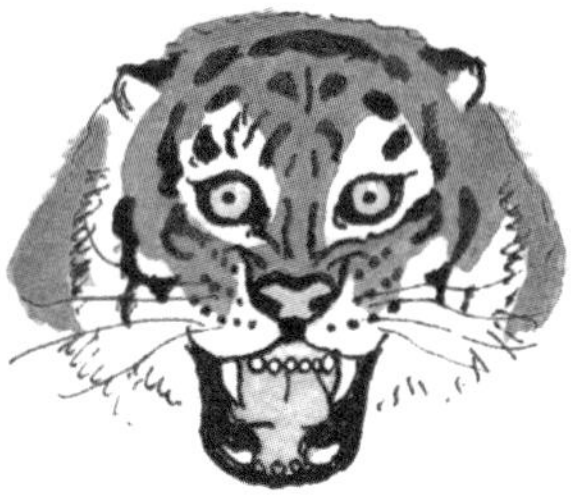

## Siberian Tiger

CD 49 • MIDI 18

**Boldly, rather fast**

FJH222

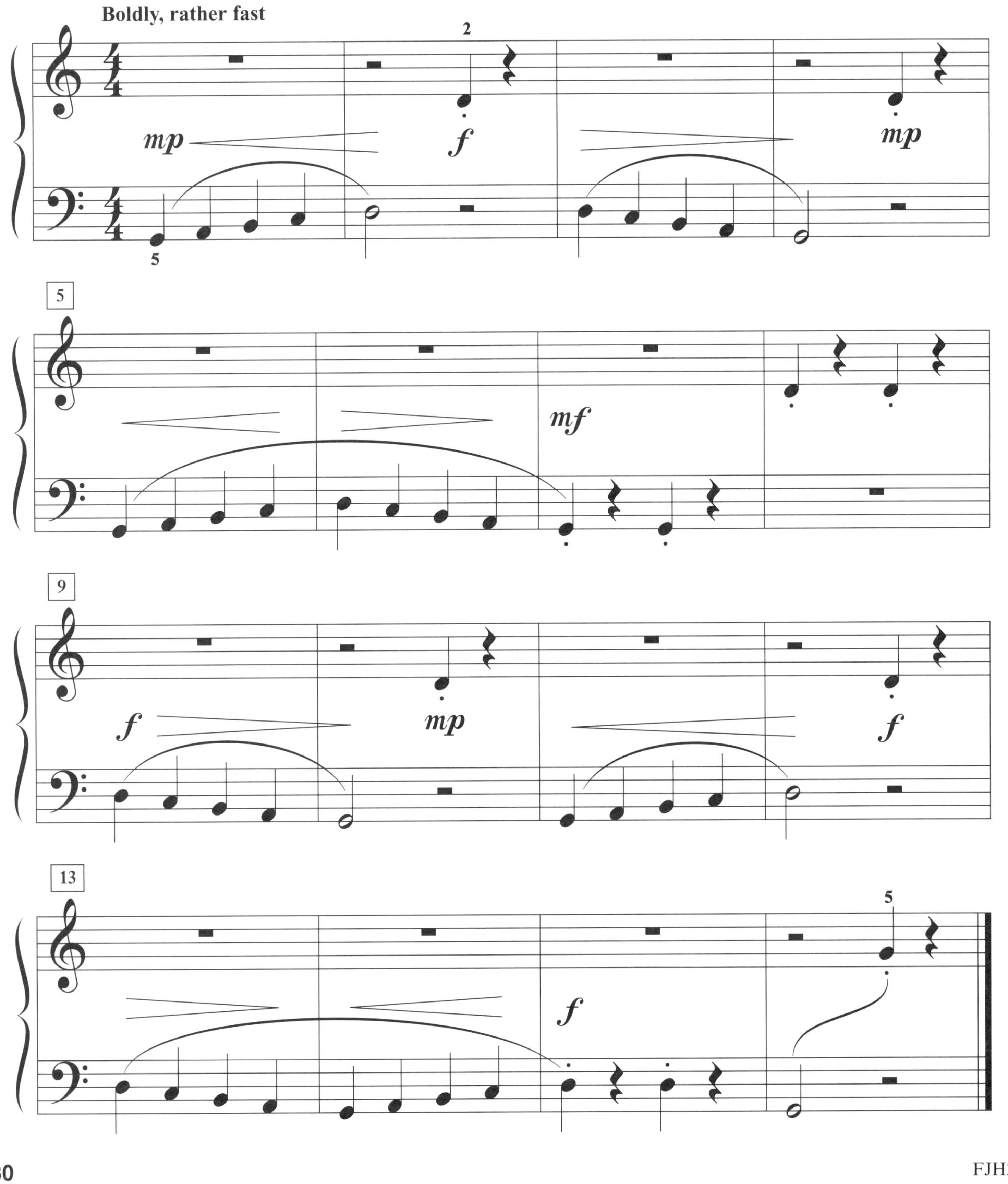

**Practice step:**

- Circle every Bass G.

CD 50, 51, 52 • MIDI 19

# Pinocchio

**Moving along**

*mf* My name is Pin - oc - chi - o, I am a wood - en boy. Al -

though Ge - pet - to made me, I'm not like oth - er toys. I

move a - round, I talk out loud, I e - ven sing a song; And

ev - 'ry time I tell a lie my nose grows two feet long!

Push forward
and off the key,
wrist first.

# Upbeat

Some pieces begin on another beat besides beat 1.
An *upbeat* is a note that comes before the first full measure.

## Practice step:

• Find and circle the upbeat in this piece.
  Notice that the 3 beats in the last measure
  plus the beat at the beginning equal 4!

## Be Upbeat!

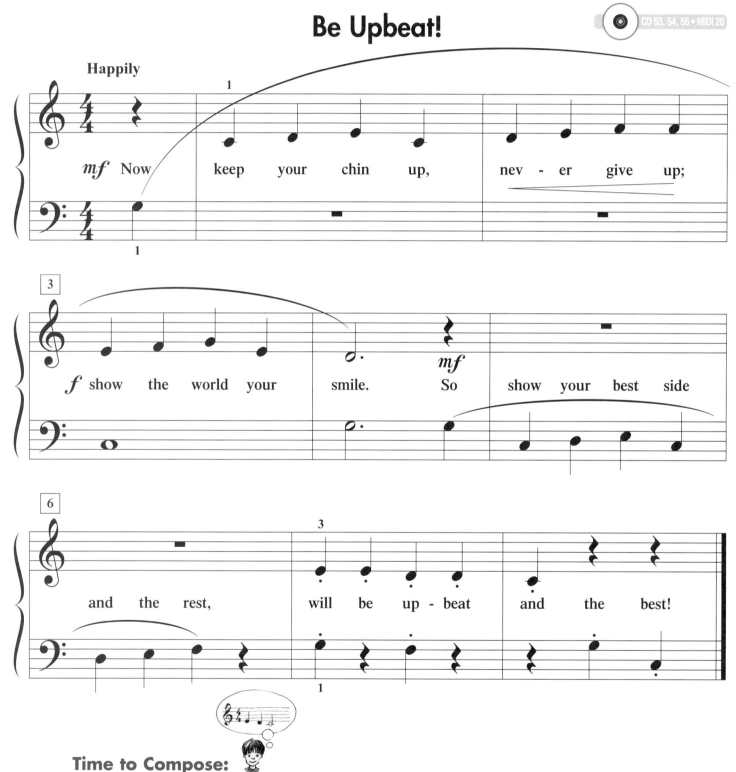

### Time to Compose:

• Make up your own piece using an upbeat. Call it "Hello!"

FJH2226

## Practice steps:

- The piece begins on beat:
  1  2  3  4  (circle one)
- Tap and count aloud.

CD 56, 57, 58 • MIDI 21

# When the Saints Go Marching In

Lively march beat

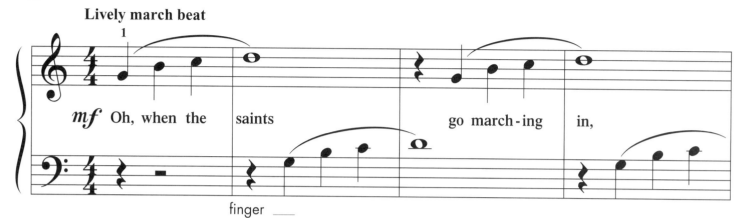

*mf* Oh, when the saints go march-ing in,

finger _____

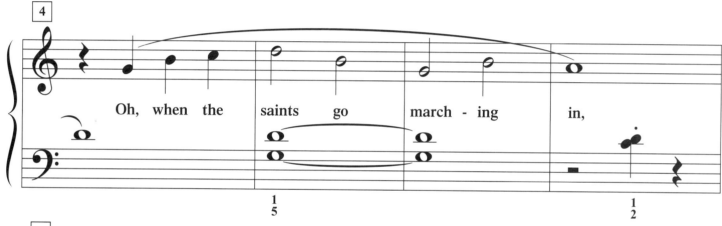

Oh, when the saints go march - ing in,

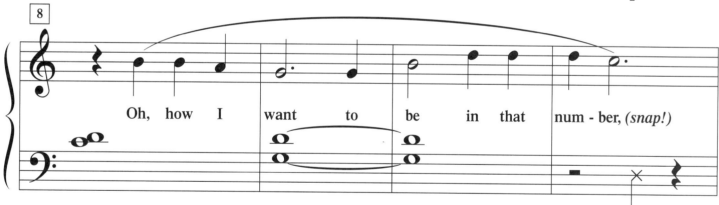

Oh, how I want to be in that num - ber, *(snap!)*

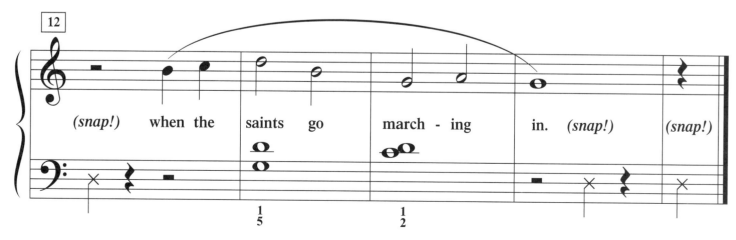

*(snap!)* when the saints go march - ing in. *(snap!)* *(snap!)*

# The C Five-Finger Pattern and the I Chord

Let's learn the C five-finger pattern and chord today!

Papa Haydn

**1.** Play a C five-finger pattern, followed by a C chord.
A chord is built using notes 1, 3, and 5 of the five-finger pattern.

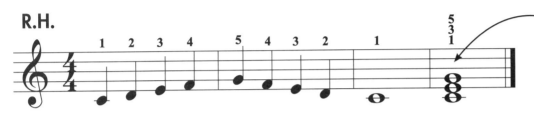

**R.H.**

This C chord is **blocked**, because all 3 notes are played together.

**2.** Now play it with your left hand.

**L.H.**

The C chord is also called the I (one) chord, or tonic chord.

**3.** When notes of the chord are played separately, they are called **broken** chords.
There are 7 broken chords below.
Circle the only **blocked** C chord.

## Waves at the Shore

**Steadily flowing**

*plan your move*

$p$

$mp$

• Notice your 8 knuckles. They look like small hills.

FJH2226

## Practice steps:

- Which line of music below has C **blocked** chords? _____
- Which line of music below has C **broken** chords? _____

*CD 60 • MIDI 23*

## Two Penguins

**Brightly**

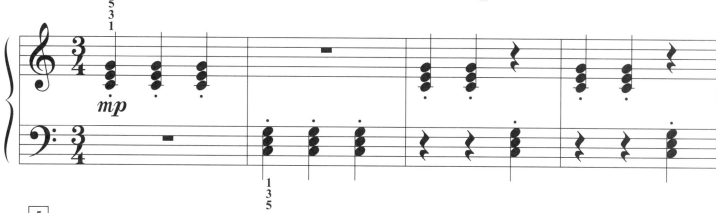

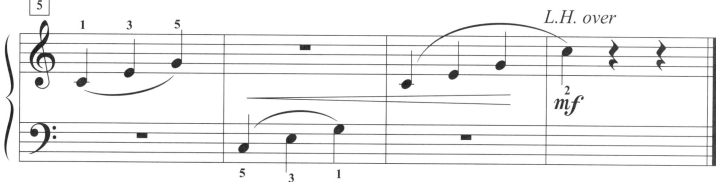

*L.H. over*

Place a check next to each technique point you did:
1. I saw four little hills in each hand. _____
2. I played with a natural "C" shape between fingers 1 and 2. _____
3. My wrist and forearm were level with each other. _____

**Check!**
Natural
"C" shape!

*CD 61 • MIDI 24*

## The C Warm-up

**Moderately fast**

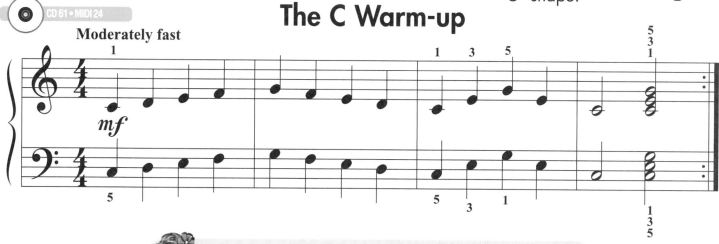

Experiment with the sound! Play the C warm-up:
- *Staccato* _____
- *Legato* _____
- At different tempos—*adagio, andante, moderato, allegro* (Cross out each tempo after you play it.)
- With different dynamics _____

JH2226

35

## Practice steps:

- Play only the blocked chords.
- Then play the broken chords followed by the cross-overs.

 CD 62, 63, 64 • MIDI 25

# The Thunderstorm

DUET PART: (student plays 1 octave higher)

FJH222

# The I and V7 Chords

As you know, tonic and dominant are two important notes.

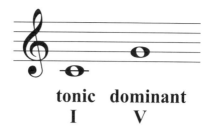

tonic    dominant
I        V

Mozart

Here is a dominant 7th chord:
It's also called a **five-seven chord**.

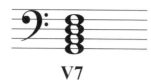

V7

To make it easier to play,
You'll see this in your music:

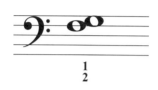     and

## Practice steps:

- Tap the rhythm.
- Practice this warm-up with your left hand:

I        V7        I

Now try it with
your R.H.

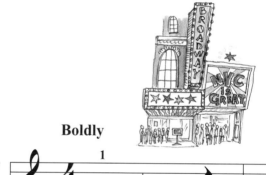

# See the Show

(F. Beyer – adapted)

CD 65, 66, 67 • MIDI 26

**Boldly**

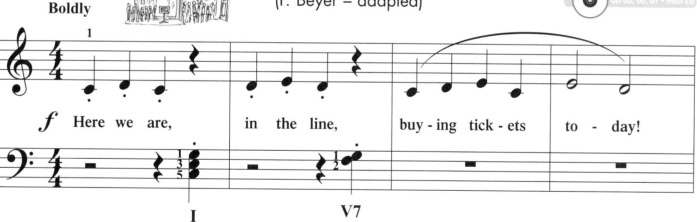

$f$ Here we are,    in the line,    buy-ing tick-ets    to - day!

I                   V7

We can't wait    'til it's time    for this show on    Broad - way!

## Practice steps:

- Find all the I (**one**) chords and then all the V7 (**five-seven**) chords.
- Write a I or a V7 in the circles.

# Dancing on the Keys

CD 68, 69, 70 • MIDI 27

**Waltzing with energy**

*f* My fin - gers dance all o - ver the keys,

*p* smooth - ly they glide and they play with such ease!

*mf* They like to waltz a - round as they *f* play,

they like to dance ev - 'ry day!

FJH22

# Accents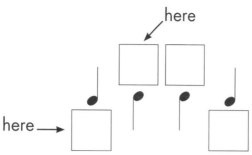

An **accent mark** means to play a note more loudly than the other notes around it.

• Draw accent marks on top or below these notes:

here →

here →

• Speak the words while clapping the rhythm.
Make the notes with accents louder than the other notes.

## Splish! Splash!

Splashing steadily

Splish!    Splash!    Walk - ing  through   pud  -  dles.

**5** Splish!    Splash!    My,    did    it    pour!

**9** Moth - er  says,  "Will  you  please  walk  'round  the    pud  -  dles?"

**13** I    say,    "Where   are   some   more?"    Splish!

## Practice step:

- Practice the measures with accents first.

 CD 71, 72, 73 • MIDI 28

# Splish and Splash

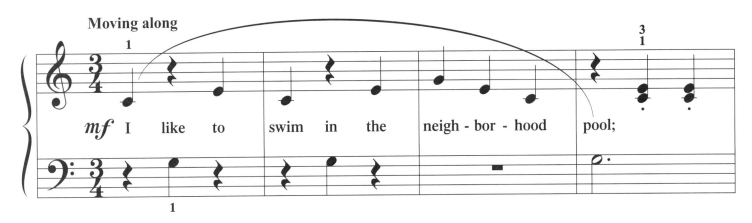

Moving along

mf  I   like   to   swim   in   the   neigh - bor - hood   pool;

f  Sum - mer's   so   hot   and   I   like   to   feel   cool.

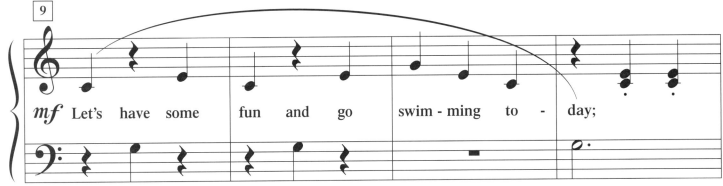

mf  Let's   have   some   fun   and   go   swim - ming   to - day;

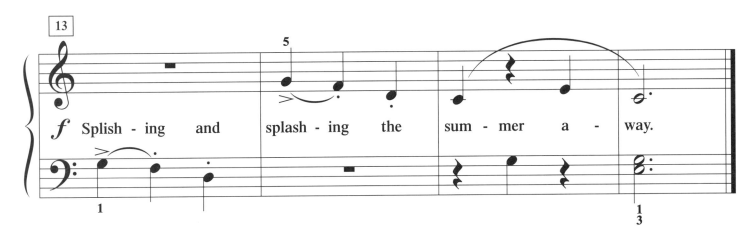

f  Splish - ing   and   splash - ing   the   sum - mer   a - way.

40

## Practice step:

- Write a I or a V7 in the circles.

CD 74, 75, 76 • MIDI 29

# The Bat

DUET PART: (student plays as written)

# The G Five-Finger Pattern and the I Chord

Let's learn the G five-finger pattern and chord today!

Beethoven

CD 77 • MIDI 30

**1.** Play a G five-finger pattern, followed by a G chord.
Remember to look for your 8 〰️〰️ .

Play R.H. alone,
then L.H. alone.
Then, hands together!

**2.**

## Big Waves

Swiftly

*mf*

*plan your move*

*(pedal optional)*

**3.**

Playfully

## Snowmen

*mp* G chords look like | snow - men! | Lis - ten to their | sound.

**Note to Teachers:** For *Snowmen*, have students lightly spring up from the keys, wrist and forearm level.
This is a "Kick Off" touch release. Remind students to play on the outside tip of their thumbnails.

FJH2226

# The I and V7 Chords

**Practice step:**

- At times, one note of the I chord is left out. It is still a I chord. Circle an example of this below.

## Trumpet Tune
### Henry Purcell

CD 78, 79, 80 • MIDI 31

- Which 2 lines of music are exactly the same? Place a ✓ in front of each of them.

## Practice steps:

- Name the ♭ in this piece: _____ ♭
- Name the ♯ in this piece: _____ ♯

CD 81, 82, 83 • MIDI 32

# Why Can't I Be a Spy?

Sneakily

*mp* Why can't I   be   a   spy?   So ex-cit-ing,   why can't I?

*mf* I'm dis-creet   on   the   street;   I   can   be   so   *p* sneak-y!

DUET PART: (student plays 1 octave higher)

R.H.
L.H.

*p*
*Play both hands 8va lower throughout*

*mp*                                                      *pp*

FJH222

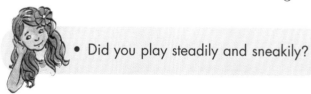
- Did you play steadily and sneakily?

## Practice steps:

- Find the patterns that are the same.
- Circle the V7 chords.
- Practice by "units"—1 measure plus 1 downbeat.

**CD 84, 85, 86 • MIDI 33**

# Blues Monster

**Time to Compose:**

- Make up your own piece only using I and V7 chords.
- Play high, low, and in the middle of the keyboard.

46

FJH2

# Music Dictionary

| Music term | Definition | Found on page: |
|---|---|---|
| accents | play more loudly than the other notes around it | 39 |
| chord | a group of three or more notes sounding together | 34 |
| downbeat | the first note of every measure | 12 |
| dynamics *p, mp, mf, f* | different degrees of softness and loudness | 3 |
| *crescendo* | means to gradually get louder (stronger) | |
| *descrescendo, diminuendo* | means to gradually get softer | 30 |
| flat sign ♭ | play the *very next key* lower | 13 |
| half step | the distance from one key to the very next key (white or black) | 9 |
| interval | the distance between any two keys | 4 |
| *legato* | (leh-GAH-toh) an Italian word that means to play smoothly | 4 |
| sharp sign # | play the *very next key* higher | 8 |
| slur | play the notes as smoothly as possible | 3 |
| *staccato* | (stah-KAH-toh) an Italian word that means to play with a detached and separated sound | 4 |
| *tempo* | an Italian word that means the speed of a piece | 6 |

*Andante*—walking speed     *Moderato*—moderate speed

*Allegro*—happy, spirited     *Adagio*—slowly

| | | |
|---|---|---|
| theme | an important melody | 15 |
| tonic and dominant | the two most important notes in a five-finger pattern. Tonic (I) is the first note. Dominant (V) is the fifth note | 24 |
| upbeat | the beat (or beats) that occurs before the first full measure of a piece | 32 |

# Certificate of Achievement

_____

Student

## has completed the

# ALL-IN-ONE APPROACH

## to Helen Marlais'
## Succeeding at the Piano®

# BOOK 1B

## You are now ready for

# BOOK 2A

_____    _____

Date                    Teacher's Signature

THE
F·J·H
MUSIC
COMPANY
INC.

Frank J. Hackinson